Fatima

The Play

Beverley Cains

Connor Court Publishing

FATIMA
THE PLAY

Beverley Cains

Published in 2017 by Connor Court Publishing Pty Ltd

Connor Court Publishing Pty Ltd
PO Box 7257
Redland Bay QLD 4165

sales@connorcourt.com
www.connorcourt.com
Phone 0497 900 685

ISBN: 9781925501636

Front Cover Design: Maria Giordano

Front Cover Photo: Catherine and Damien Newton

Printed in Australia

DEDICATION

I dedicate this play to my husband Kevin and our wonderful family. Support for all my endeavours, has come from all of them. In particular I must thank Cathy and Damien for the photos and Anne for editing and the tedious work of proof reading. Special thanks to the grandchildren who feature in the photos- Ellen, Thomas, Eloise and Amelia.

Thanks also to my dear friends from north Queensland, for assisting in finding the Herberton "Hail Mary" and clarifying memories.

PRAISE FOR FATIMA THE PLAY

Fatima, The Play written by Beverley Cains is an excellent example of how to employ the art of theatre in the propagation of the message from Fatima.

Whilst many of the older generation would be quite familiar with the story of Fatima, this play is written in such a way that an audience of children and adolescents are able to place themselves beside the three children; Lucia, Francisco and Jacinta as they discover Our Lady and encounter the captivating events that unfolded in the Portuguese village of Fatima in 1917. The inclusion of a modern day child asking questions to a Priest throughout the play makes for an almost dialogue-like audience interaction with many key points of the play being highlighted along the way.

The children's dialogue amongst each other throughout the play allows the audience to experience the events of Fatima in the same childlike way that the three children were able to. The audience are ready to weep and rejoice with the children as they meet Our Lady face to face whilst truly coming to a realisation of what an amazing miracle this truly was.

This play is particularly important this year, the 100th anniversary of Apparitions of the Blessed Mother to the three shepherd-children: Lucia, Francesco and Jacinta, of which the two latter are the newest and the youngest saints of the Catholic Church. It is a call for the renewal of interest in Our Lady's requests and the effects of her apparitions which are still resounding throughout the world, even today. *Fatima, The Play* by Beverley Cains not only accommodates that call of re-examination, but brings the story of Fatima to the future generations of the Catholic Church. My hope is that parishes and schools, where this play is performed, will be inspired to enter the school of Our Lady, where She, the Teacher in the Spirit, shows us how to love God even more.

Fr. Damian Mosakowski, osppe
Rector of the Diocesan Shrine of Our Lady of Mercy - Penrose Park

INTRODUCTION

The excitement of the centenary of the apparitions of the Virgin Mary to three young children at Fatima, in Portugal (May – October 2017) has propelled me to attempt to retell this simple story in a play for upper Primary or Middle School children. In the 1950's in Australia the Father Patrick Peyton campaign was a boost for praying the Rosary and by implication, Fatima, and the beautiful lady who said "I am the Lady of the Rosary." The slogan "The Family that Prays together, Stays together" resounded well. Since then, the cult of the Virgin Mary has been rather subdued.

The wonderful children of Year Six at Holy Trinity School, Curtin in the Australian Capital Territory, were so excited when they were offered the opportunity to workshop this play, in June 2016. Their enthusiasm convinced me that the interest was there to attempt to take this project a step further to reveal some of the treasures of the Blessed Virgin Mary; some new approaches to prayer and suffering for this young and willing generation, and to whoever would see their performance.

In the early 1950's, I participated in a college production of a Fatima play which was written by a Sister or Sisters of Mercy who conducted Mt. St. Bernard College, in Herberton, North Queensland. This Fatima play did not have the trappings of a modern, sophisticated production – the theatre could have been called a bush theatre - the story itself was the wonder; great devotion and praise for the Mother of God. The fervour of the actors gave their audience something to remember. Perhaps there could be another Fatima play coming out of Australia for the great centenary.

The nineteenth century saw anti-clericalism raise its head in Portugal. By the end of that century the situation improved but a new wave of anti-Clericalism came with the Portuguese First republic in 1910. As part of the anti-clerical revolution, the bishops were driven from their dioceses, the property of clerics was seized by the state, wearing of the clerical attire in the street was banned, most seminaries were closed.[1] Religious orders were expelled from the country, including 31 orders comprising members in 164 houses; religious education was prohibited in both primary and secondary school. Religious oaths and church taxes were also abolished.[2]

Portugal remained neutral until April 1916 when Germany declared war. Despite

---

[1] 1981, German, English Book Edition: *History of the Church* /Ed Jedin, Dolan *Vol 10 The Church in the modern age*/ by Gabriel Adrianyl (et al.) translated by Anselm Biggs. p. 612.
[2] Ibid.

the deprivations of war and the restrictions of the republican government, many citizens were faithful to the Church especially peasants and subsistent farmers. In the Serra da Aire, the small village of Fatima, the Church of St. Anthony had a Parish Priest and the faith of the previous centuries was alive and celebrated.

In Fatima, the Angel of Portugal had visited Lucia dos Santos and her two cousins Francisco and Jacinto Marto during the summer of 1916 twice and then for a third time, in October. There was something from God "which impressed the words on our minds, yet (as well) a voice of authority"[3]which convinced us not to reveal these experiences. By May 1917, family members, brothers and cousins and friends were off to the war and a general air of sadness pervaded village life. Europe was "in the grip of the cruel war, the suicide of Europe"[4]; Pope Benedict XV wrote his letter which introduced the title, Mary Queen of Peace to the Loreto Litany of the Blessed Virgin. Within weeks the Lady of the Rosary was in Fatima to deliver her message which would bring Peace and her request for Prayer and Penance, which if heeded, would save the world from the scourge of Communism and another world war.

I am indebted to William Thomas Walsh, outstanding and versatile writer who researched and interviewed many of the participants in this drama who wrote "Our Lady of Fatima" first published by The MacMillan Company in 1947. Later published by Image in 1954 and 1990. This book has been my companion for many years.

In the play we see the Village Square filled with dancing, a religious procession and crowning of the Virgin Mary's statue near the small market place; we meet the families of the children and some of their siblings; the local (anti Catholic) Mayor kidnaps the children; we observe the pilgrims arriving and hushed at the Cova da Iria. The play is flexible to include a modest number of performers but with the influx of pilgrims and a choir there is the potential for a larger number of performers to be involved. There are two Narrators and a present day Father Joseph who accompanies a local child, Samuel or Samantha, to answer Sam's questions which are those of the modern day audience – "Is she a visitor from outer space?"

The play would run for about ninety minutes with one interval.

---

[3] *Our Lady of Fatima*, William Thomas Walsh, Image edition published May 1990; ISBN 0-385-02869-5 p. 44.

[4] Ibid., p. 49.

FATIMA CHARACTERS

OUR LADY OF FATIMA

ANGEL OF PORTUGAL

DOS SANTOS FAMILY

LUCIA: 10 years

MARIA ROSA: mother

GLORIA: older sister

MARIA OF THE ANGELS: older sister

MARTO FAMILY

OLIMPIA: mother

ANTONIO (TI): father

FRANCISCO: 9 years

JACINTA: 7 years

JOHN: 11 years

ANNA: 12/13yrs

NARRATORS: 1 AND 2

FATHER JOE: Catholic Priest (perhaps a Franciscan)

SAMUEL (SAM) OR SAMANTHA (SAM) - Local child – could be in school uniform.

MAYOR OF PROVINCE

FATHER MANUEL FERREIRA: Parish Priest

PILGRIMS: Rich Portuguese, peasants and others. Visiting Clergy and Religious for apparitions.

PILGRIMS: Peasants are dressed simply – women with black shawls covering shoulders and heads – often black or dark dresses. Men wear working boots and the suits- Mass suits for Sunday Mass. Children with scarves or hats and aprons, often. Women sometimes carry shoes; many peasants are without shoes.

RICH PILGRIMS: Women in long skirts and large hats and men with high collars, vests and hats.

CLERGY: Black soutane and black hats.

ACT 1, SCENE 1 - FRONT STAGE

ENTER FATHER JOE AND SAMUEL OR SAMANTHA A LOCAL CHILD

FATHER JOE: Hello there, everyone. I am a Catholic Priest and today I want to tell you a special story. It is a true story about Mary, the Mother of Jesus. Have you heard of this special woman, Sam?

SAM: Yes, her name is Mary and we sometimes say she is "Our Lady."

FATHER JOE: Yes, and we often see nice pictures of Mary with Jesus. In this story Mary goes to a country called Portugal to visit three children.

SAM: Sounds a bit like a visitor from outer space to me!

FATHER JOE: No Sam, Our Lady is a visitor from Heaven.

SAM: I know that Angels come from Heaven. Does she bring any Angels with her?

FATHER JOE: Well yes and no. Sam - there is an Angel in the story… the Angel comes to visit the children to get them ready for the visit of Our Lady. (MOVING TO EXIT) The story begins in a small village in Portugal in 1916. A village called Fatima.

SAM: Is it a true story? (SAM AND FATHER JOE PROCEED TOWARDS EXIT.)

FATHER JOE: Oh yes. Amazing and TRUE. Most of our story happened just one hundred years ago. It was a difficult time because of the war. And this war had been going on for a long time. (EXIT)

NARRATOR 1:   The people of St. Anthony's Parish in Fatima celebrated many feasts. Of course there were great Christmas and Easter celebrations.

NARRATOR 2: In May they came together for Mass to Honour Our Lady. So let us see how the people celebrated after Mass in May 1916. We will join the dancers in front of the Church near the market.

EXIT AS MUSIC COMMENCES.

ACT 1, SCENE 2 - MAIN SQUARE FATIMA

JOYFUL OPENING WITH CHILDREN IN VILLAGE SQUARE DANCING PORTUGUESE FOLK DANCE. THERE ARE PAIRS OF DANCERS, GIRLS WITH RED SCARVES ON THEIR HEADS AND RED APRONS OVER DARK SKIRTS AND WHITE BLOUSES, BOYS WITH WHITE SHIRTS AND DARK TROUSERS. DANCING TO ONE SIDE OF THE STAGE. MARKET STALLS ACROSS THE STAGE WITH VILLAGERS PASSING THROUGH. MARKET STALLS SHOW LOCAL PRODUCE – POTATOES, ONIONS AND SIMPLE VEGETABLES AND SOME FRUIT. MAYBE SOME FLOWERS/RUSH BROOMS.

DANCING FINISHES AS THE CHOIR IS HEARD AND THE PROCESSION BEGINS. A STATUE OF THE VIRGIN MARY IS CARRIED ON A FLOWER-DECKED BIER BY SOME OF THE BOYS. 4 OR 6 BOYS STOP, LOWER THE STATUE AND A GROUP OF GIRLS IN WHITE WITH VEILS COME AS THE SINGING CONTINUES. THE GIRLS GROUP AROUND AS THE FINAL GIRL COMES FORWARD AND CROWNS THE STATUE WITH A FLORAL CROWN. THE BOYS CARRYING THE BIER COME FORWARD AND THE PROCESSION CONTINUES AROUND THE STAGE AND PROCEEDS THROUGH A DOOR - APPROPRIATELY NOTED AS THE CHURCH DOOR INTO THE CHURCH WHERE ALL EXIT THE STAGE.

ACT 1, SCENE 3 - PASTORAL SCENE - SHEEP FIELDS

PASTORAL SCENE. LUCIA, FRANCISCO AND JACINTA ARE IN THE FIELDS WITH THE SHEEP. CHILDREN ARE PLAYING AND GATHERING STICKS. ANGELUS BELL RINGS: CHILDREN STOP TO PRAY. SAY PRAYERS QUIETLY. RESUME CHATTING AND PLAYING.

JACINTA: Maria da Silva crowned the Virgin Mary's statue this year, Lucia. I wish I could crown Our Lady next year.

FRANCISCO: You're much too small. You would never reach high enough to put the crown on Our Lady's head. (JACINTA REACTS TO FRANCISCO.)

LUCIA: (KINDLY) Maybe next year Jacinta you will grow especially if you don't get the cold again in winter.

FRANCISCO: Let's enjoy the sunshine while we can…. (SUDDEN STRONG WIND) Where is the wind coming from all of a sudden? And look at that light in the distance …it's getting closer, it's coming towards us.

LIGHT APPEARS IN THE DISTANCE AND GROWS STRONGER AS IT APPROACHES GROWS LARGER AND COMES BEFORE THEM IN THE SHAPE OF A BEAUTIFUL ANGEL.

ANGEL: Do not be afraid. I am the Angel of Peace. Pray with me.

ANGEL PROSTRATES ON THE GROUND; CHILDREN FOLLOW, AS IN A DAZE, AND PROSTRATE NEAR THE ANGEL

ANGEL: My God, I believe, I adore, I hope and I love you. I beg pardon of
                    you for those who do not believe, do not adore, do not hope and
                    do not love you.

ALL 3 CHILDREN REPEAT THE ANGEL'S WORDS: "My God, I believe, I
adore, I hope and I love you. I beg pardon for those who do not believe, do not adore,
do not hope and do not love you." (PAUSE) "My God, I believe…"

ANGEL (RISING FROM GROUND AND SAYS VERY CLEARLY):   This is
how to pray: the hearts of Jesus and Mary are listening to your voices.[5]
ANGEL MELTS INTO THE SUN. CHILDREN STAY DOWN. FRANCISCO
GETS UP SLOWLY AND SITS NEARBY.

FRANCISCO: I can't stay down all this time.

LUCIA, JACINTA & FRANCISCO: My God, I believe, I adore, I hope and I love
you. I beg pardon of you for those who do not believe, do not adore, do not hope
and do not love you. (PAUSE)

GIRLS STAND AND NO ONE SAYS ANYTHING. THEY WALK AS IF IN A
DREAM OFF STAGE.

MID CURTAIN CLOSES.

---

[5] Ibid., p. 36.

ACT 1, SCENE 4 - FRONT OF CURTAIN

FATHER JOE AND SAM ENTER.

SAM: Did those children really see the Angel?

FATHER JOE: Oh yes, they did. Did you know you have a Guardian Angel? And
                - there is an angel protecting your school. (PAUSE) These were
                special children being prepared for something amazing. I wonder
                if we can all (GESTURING TO AUDIENCE) say the prayer
                again now – My God, I believe, I adore, I hope and I love you. I
                beg pardon of you for those who do not believe, do not adore, do
                not hope and do not love you.

FATHER JOE AND SAM MOVE TO SIDE OF STAGE AS CURTAIN OPENS.

NARRATOR 1:   Time passes. It is now August 1916. Summer is very hot but our
                little shepherds are trying to cool off.

NARRATOR 2:   The children were sitting by the well in the shade of the fig tree
                near the house. Suddenly they turn to the voice.

WIND AND LIGHT FOR THE ANGEL'S APPEARANCE. QUICKLY

ANGEL: What are you doing? Pray! Pray a great deal. The hearts of Jesus
                and of Mary have plans for all of you. Offer prayer and sacrifices
                constantly to God.[6]

LUCIA: Please help us to understand how we must we make sacrifices?

ANGEL: You must try to be kind to others. Sometimes sharing your time to
                help others. Even sharing your food. Offer sacrifices for sinners
                and pray for the conversion of sinners. You will help peace to come
                to your country. I am its Guardian Angel, the Angel of Portugal.
                Above all, accept and put up with all the suffering which the Lord
                will send you.

---

[6] Ibid., p. 37.

ANGEL LEAVES. MID CURTAIN CLOSES AND CHILDREN STAY IN PLACE.

FATHER JOE & SAM FROM THE SIDE OF STAGE:

FATHER JOE: Towards the end of the year, the Angel visits the children again.

MID CURTAIN OPENS AS THE CHILDREN FINISH PRAYERS.

THIRD VISIT FROM THE ANGEL.

THE CHILDREN FINISH THE ROSARY AND THEY SAY THE PRAYER:

LUCIA, JACINTA AND FRANCISCO: "Holy Mary Mother of God, pray for us sinners now and at the hour of our death. Amen. My God, I believe, I adore, I hope and I love you. I beg pardon of you for those who not believe, do not adore, and do not hope and do not love you."

LIGHT COMES SWIFTLY ACROSS THE VALLEY. ANGEL APPEARS WITH A CHALICE AND OVER THE CHALICE, A HOST IS SUSPENDED. THESE MYSTICAL OBJECTS REMAIN SUSPENDED WHILE THE ANGEL PROSTRATES HIMSELF ON THE GROUND AND SAYS:

ANGEL: Most Holy Trinity, Father, Son, and Holy Spirit, I adore you profoundly and offer you the Body, Blood, Soul and Divinity of Jesus Christ.[7] I offer this prayer to make up for the terrible sins that offend Jesus. Let us pray to the Sacred Heart of Jesus and Immaculate Heart of Mary for the conversion of sinners.
ANGEL DISTRIBUTES SACRED HOST TO LUCIA WHILST JACINTA AND FRANCISCO SIP FROM THE CHALICE
Receive the Body and Blood of Jesus. Console Our Lord and pray for all sinners.

THE CHILDREN STAY DOWN, IN PRAYER, AS THE CURTAIN CLOSES.

---

[8] Ibid., p. 41.

ACT 1, SCENE 5 - FRONT OF CURTAIN

FATHER JOE AND SAM COME TO CENTRE STAGE. THEY MAY BE SITTING ON A STONE OR SITTING ON A SMALL SEAT AS CURTAIN OPENS.

FATHER JOE: The children are becoming more careful with their prayers and they are praying often.

SAM: Did they tell anyone about the visits of the Angel?

FATHER JOE: No, they just felt they could not tell anyone.

SAM: No one at all?

FATHER JOE: They spoke to each other about the Angel and they often said the Angel's prayer but they did not tell anyone about the visits of the Angel. I suppose they thought no one would believe them.

SAM: (DEFINITELY) It was true...the Angel did visit them three times.

FATHER JOE: Yes Sam. They spoke about what the Angel may have meant when he asked them to bear the suffering God may send them. They did not really understand what suffering the Angel might be talking about. But the visits of the Angel were their very special secret.

SAM: They did keep that to themselves. (SAM AND FATHER JOE EXIT.)

ACT 1, SCENE 6 - VILLAGE SQUARE FATIMA

SUGGEST DANCERS AND PROCESSION, OR JUST THE PROCESSION. COULD BE A SHORTER REPEAT OF THE OPENING SCENE BUT WITHOUT THE MARKET-PLACE SET-UP.

THIS PASSAGE BY NARRATORS FROM THE SIDE OF THE STAGE AS THE DANCING AND PROCESSION PROCEED.

NARRATOR 1:   We are now moving ahead to May 1917 and another procession and crowning of Our Lady is occurring. It is the 13th May, 1917. The war continues in parts of Europe but the villages of Portugal are not much changed.

NARRATOR 2:   Some young men have gone to the battlefields but life in Fatima and other small villages continues. The people work long hours during the week and go to Mass on Sundays and feast days.

NARRATORS 1 and 2:   Here we are in the village square in front of St. Anthony's church in Fatima. (EXCITEDLY) Look, just look at the sweet child crowning the Virgin Mary! Jacinta Marto!

AS OPENING SCENE: DANCING FOLLOWED BY PROCESSION AND CROWNING OF THE VIRGIN MARY'S STATUE, BY JACINTA MARTO. A HYMN TO THE VIRGIN MARY IS SUNG DURING THE CROWNING.

SCENE CHANGES QUICKLY.

ACT 1, SCENE 7 - OUTSIDE MARTO FAMILY HOME

OUTSIDE MARTO FAMILY HOME AS FRANCISCO AND JACINTA COLLECT THEIR LUNCH AND PROCEED TO GATHER THE ANIMALS TO GO ON THE ROAD TO THE COVA DA IRA. THEY MEET UP WITH LUCIA AS THEY PROCEED.

OLIMPIA: Here is your lunch. You will meet Lucia as you go.

FRANCISCO: Thanks, Mumma. Cinta is not far behind. She was so happy to crown Our Lady!

OLIMPIA: You keep an eye on your little sister, please. JACINTA RUNS TO MEET THEM.

FRANCISCO AND JACINTA: See you later, Mumma. 'Bye.

OLIMPIA: 'Bye bye. There's Lucia just ahead.

COVA DA IRA: SHEEP GRAZING PEACEFULLY.

ACT 1, SCENE 8 - COVA DA IRIA

LUCIA: The sheep seem happy - let's play for a while.

FRANCISCO: Yes - can we build a small house with these rocks?

JACINTA: We will say the Rosary later.

THEY SET ABOUT MOVING ROCKS, BUILDING UP THINGS WHEN A SUDDEN BRIGHT FLASH OF LIGHT STARTLES THEM.

JACINTA: What was that? We better get to some cover before it rains.

THEY RUSH TO SEEK COVER FROM A TREE. ANOTHER FLASH AND THEY GO TO MOVE AGAIN BUT THEY SEE A BALL OF LIGHT ON THE TOP OF A SMALL OAK TREE IN THE MIDST OF THE LIGHT STOOD A LADY, CLOUD AROUND HER FEET.

OUR LADY: Don't be afraid. I won't hurt you.[8] (THE CHILDREN, STANDING, DRAW NEARER AND BECOME ATTENTIVE.)

LUCIA: Where does Your Excellency come from?

OUR LADY: I am from Heaven.

LUCIA: And what is it you want of me and my cousins?

OUR LADY: I am here to ask you to come to this Cova for the next six months on the thirteenth day at this same time. Then I will tell you who I am, and what I want. And afterwards I will return here a seventh time.

LUCIA: Shall I go to heaven one day?

---

[9] Ibid., p.51.

OUR LADY: Yes you will.

LUCIA: And Jacinta?

OUR LADY: (NODDING) Yes.

LUCIA: and Francisco?

OUR LADY: Yes, yes. But he will have to say many Rosaries!

LUCIA: Is little Maria da Neves now in heaven?

OUR LADY: Yes she is (NODDING)

LUCIA: And Amelia - Amelia she was only 19 or 20 years old?

OUR LADY: She will be in purgatory for a long time! But she will get to Heaven then. (PAUSE) Do you wish to offer yourselves to God and pray with patience during any suffering that He may decide to send you? This would be an act of reparation for the sins which offend Him so much.

LUCIA AND JACINTA: Yes we do.

OUR LADY: And will you pray and ask for the conversion of sinners?

LUCIA AND JACINTA: Yes, we will.

OUR LADY: Then you will have to suffer. (PAUSE) Suffering can be a *very* special kind of prayer. (PAUSE) Suffering is sometimes hard, sometimes very hard, but the grace of God will be your comfort.

OUR LADY OPENS HER HANDS AND THE LIGHT INTENSIFIES. THE CHILDREN FALL TO THEIR KNEES AND COVER THEIR FACES AS THEY SAY:

LUCIA/FRANCISCO/JACINTA: "O most Holy Trinity, I adore You! Jesus, My God, I love you in the Most Blessed Sacrament!"[9]

GRADUALLY THEY REGAIN COMPOSURE AND LOOK TOWARDS OUR LADY STILL KNEELING.

OUR LADY: Please say the Rosary every day, to obtain peace for the world and the end of the war.

OUR LADY BEGINS TO RISE FROM THE TREE AND GLIDE AWAY TOWARDS THE EAST. THE CHILDREN STARE INTO THE DISTANCE AND STAND GAZING.

JACINTA: Oh, such a pretty Lady. Oh so pretty. Did you hear Francisco?

FRANCISCO: No I did not hear, but I saw the beautiful Lady. What did she say? Please tell me what the beautiful Lady said.

JACINTA: She said we would all go to Heaven, but you must say many, many Rosaries.

FRANCISCO: I will, I will, oh my dear Lady – I will say all the Rosaries you want.

JACINTA: Oh what a beautiful lady.

LUCIA: Yes she is very beautiful but you must keep her visit as a secret – just as we kept the visits of the Angel a secret.

JACINTA AND FRANCISCO: Yes we will. We will, we will.

LUCIA: Well, my dear cousins. This is very important. (DRAWING THE TWO YOUNGER CHILDREN AROUND HER.) We must not tell anyone about this. No one at all…not even Mumma and Poppa. Do you understand? (SCEPTICALLY) It is important… do not tell anyone!

---

[9] Ibid., p. 52.

JACINTA AND FRANCISCO: I won't tell. No don't worry, I won't tell a soul. I won't tell, no I won't tell!

LUCIA PAUSES AND NODS HER HEAD, FORE-SEEING THE TROUBLES WHICH LAY AHEAD AS THEY BURST OUT AGAIN. AD LIB.

JACINTA/FRANCISCO: She had a white veil and lovely Rosary beads...all shining. She looked sad sometimes. The light was so bright. Her dress was so white and lovely.

THE CHILDREN MOVE SLOWLY WITH THEIR SHEEP TOWARDS HOME STILL CHATTING HAPPILY ABOUT THE BEAUTIFUL LADY.

SCENE CHANGES. LUCIA PASSES ACROSS THE STAGE. LUCIA APPEARS WITHOUT HER HEAD SCARF AND APRON.

ACT 1, SCENE 9 - FRONT OF CURTAIN

LUCIA: I have had my supper Mumma, I'll go to bed.

ACT 1, SCENE 10 - MARTO HOME KITCHEN

MARTO'S HOME. OLIMPIA IS PREPARING THE EVENING MEAL. JOHN AND ANNA ARE SITTING NEARBY.

JACINTA AND FRANCISCO COME IN SKIPPING AND LOOKING VERY PLEASED ABOUT SOMETHING.

OLIMPIA: You children seem a bit excited today? Are all the animals set for the night?

JACINTA AND FRANCISCO: Yes Mumma (SPEAKING TOGETHER)

JACINTA: Oh Mumma – I saw Our Lady at the Cova da Iria today.

OLIMPIA: (CHUCKLING)– Sure yes, you are such a saint, Jacinta, that Our Lady would come to see you, wouldn't she? (AS SHE CONTINUES WITH HER PREPARATION OF A MEAL.)

JACINTA: But I *saw* her (RUSHING TO HER MOTHER, TUGGING HER APRON AND SPEAKING EXCITEDLY). We saw a flash of lightning and rushed to the Cova, but as we ran we saw a bright light which came close to us *and* in the light was Our Lady. She is so beautiful. She told us to say the Rosary every day and she said we were both going heaven![10]

OLIMPIA: So you saw A lady!

FRANCISCO: No Mumma, not just A lady – Our Lady. Dressed all in white with a veil and oh so beautiful.

---

[10] Ibid., p. 54.

TI ENTERS THE ROOM, GETS A BOWL OF SOUP (FOOD) AND SITS TO
EAT.

OLIMPIA: Jacinta – Francisco – tell your father about the lady you saw today
                    in the Cova da Iria.

JACINTA: Poppa, I saw Our Lady, dressed in white today at the Cova da Ira.
                    She is so pretty.

FRANCISCO NODS HEAD IN AGREEMENT

TI: (PUTS DOWN HIS FOOD AND SPEAKS SLOWLY AND
                    SERIOUSLY TO FRANCISCO.) Francisco, come here to me.
                    Did you see the Lady?

FRANCISCO: Oh yes – she is so beautiful (SIGHING).

OLIMPIA: Fine little saints we have here! Fancy having the idea that Our Lady
                    would come to visit them!!

TI: (THOUGHTFULLY AND DELIBERATELY) Well if the
                    children did see a beautiful lady dressed in white – who else could
                    it be BUT Our Lady?

OLIMPIA: (SHOCKED) What are you saying?

TI: (IMPORTANT SPEECH. IT MUST BE CLEARLY
                    ARTICULATED AND SAID SLOWLY) For hundreds of years
                    Our Lady has come down from Heaven with messages. You know
                    all about the young girl at Lourdes. Bernadette. Our Lady came
                    to France to visit Bernadette only 50 or 60 years ago. Our Lady
                    has come to visit good people, many of them children, a number
                    of times in many different countries. God's power is great. We

don't quite understand this now, but I think it will turn out to be something.[11]

(PAUSE. CHILDREN RUSH TO HUG HIM AND HE CONTINUES) Come on, the two of you, eat your supper and get to bed.

CURTAIN

---

[11] Ibid., p.56.

ACT 1, SCENE 11 - DOS SANTOS HOME

NEXT DAY DOS SANTOS HOME: ENTER MARIA OF THE ANGELS
(LUCIA'S SISTER) AND LUCIA.

MARIA: Oh Lucia, I hear you have seen Our Lady.

LUCIA STARES IN SILENCE.

MARIA: Is it true?

LUCIA: Who told you?

MARIA: The neighbours say Jacinta told her mother all about it.

LUCIA: And I begged her not to tell anyone. (ON THE VERGE OF
                  TEARS)

MARIA: Why not tell everyone?

LUCIA: Because I don't know for sure if it was Our Lady. She was a very
                  pretty little woman.[12]

MARIA: And what did this very pretty little woman say to you?
                  (SARCASTICALLY)

LUCIA: (INNOCENTLY – SWEETLY) She wants us to go on the 13th of
                  every month for the next 6 months to the Cova da Iria. We should
                  be there when the Angelus bell rings. After the six months she will
                  tell us who she is and what she wants.

MARIA: Didn't you ask her who she was?

---

[12] Ibid., p. 56.

LUCIA: I asked her where she came from and she said, "I come from Heaven."

MARIA: Wait till I tell Mumma and Poppa this story!

CURTAIN

ACT 1, SCENE 12 - FRONT OF CURTAIN

FATHER JOE:　This was the way most people reacted when they heard the story of the visit of Our Lady to the three children.

SAM:　I wonder if anyone will believe them. (SAM EXITS PLAYING WITH A BALL OR SMALL TOY.)

NARRATOR 1:　The children tried to keep to themselves to avoid the questions and teasing of some villagers. But word quickly spread to the nearby villages.

NARRATOR 2:　And now, one month later, the great feast of St. Anthony on the thirteenth of June 1917 was a happy occasion with the usual celebrations.

ACT 1, SCENE 13 - DOS SANTOS HOME

DOS SANTOS HOME - FEAST OF ST. ANTHONY, 13 JUNE, 1917.

MARIA ROSE: Lucia – there are people outside our home, wanting to speak with you.

LUCIA: Yes, they are wanting directions to the Cove da Iria.

MARIA ROSA: But surely you are not going to the Cova today. Everyone is getting ready for St. Anthony's Feast Day. There'll be dancing and singing and don't forget the wonderful white bread – St. Anthony's bread… you love those white loves, Lucia.

LUCIA: (VERY MATTER OF FACTLY) This year after Mass I will go to Cova da Iria.

MARIA (LUCIA'S SISTER):   Oh come, Lucia, you don't really expect the lady to come.

LUCIA: It is the 13th and she said she would come again at 12 o'clock.

MARIA: You'll miss the dancing and singing and you will not see any of the decorations.

GLORIA: And you will not see any of the fireworks! You'll miss all the fun!

LUCIA: (VERY DEFINITELY) Jacinta, Francisco and I will be going to the Cova today after Mass.

MARIA ROSA: You are so stubborn – worse than your father. (PAUSE - MAY BE SOME REACTION!) I will take you to see Father Ferreira. Our Parish Priest is a sensible man. I want to get his opinion of the whole thing.

ACT 1, SCENE 14 - MARTO'S HOME

MARTO'S HOME

JACINTA: Please hurry Francisco – today is our special day.

ANNA: But you will miss the dancing, Jacinta.

JOHN: I will be staying to see the decorations and have some of the sweets.

OLIMPIA: Oh Jacinta - you seem so sure the lady will come again!

JACINTA: Yes Mumma – she will come - she promised us!

FRANCISCO: Please come with us Mumma – you may not see the beautiful lady
                but you will "feel" that she is there.

OLIMPIA: Your father and I are hoping to come. Then maybe you will stop
                telling these terrible stories. People in the villages all around Fatima,
                are all talking about us!

TI: I would love to come, but there is a cattle sale on today and I
                must buy a couple of animals at the fair across the valley. And
                Olimpia, I'm sorry, I need you to come with me. So after Mass at
                St Anthony's we will have to head off.

FRANCISCO: (VERY CLEARLY) We'll go to the Cova da Iria with Lucia, after
                Mass.

OLIMPIA: Are you telling me you will not stay for the singing and dancing?
                And Lucia too?

JACINTA: We will go after Mass to the Cova to be there for Our Lady.

OLIMPIA: (MOTHERLY) We all must hurry along now. But please do not be getting too excited - I think you are expecting too much. I would hate you to be disappointed.

ALL EXIT. JACINTA AND FRANCISCO RUSH OFF WITH THE PARENTS, JOHN AND ANNA FOLLOWING.

ACT 1, SCENE 15 - ST. ANTHONY'S CHURCH

LUCIA AND HER MOTHER GO TO SEE FATHER – OUTSIDE OF THE CHURCH DOOR.

FATHER FERREIRA: Good morning Mrs Dos Santos.

MARIA ROSA: Good morning Father. You know my daughter's crazy story. Do you think I should allow her to go to the Cova da Iria today? She is convinced there will be another visit of her lady.

FATHER FERREIRA: (NODDING) Let Lucia go. And let the cousins go too. I will see them all tomorrow to get them to tell me their story. Now, off to Mass, Lucia. (LUCIA EXITS)

FATHER FERRERIA: (VERY DELIBERATELY TO MARIA ROSA) I will get to the bottom of this tomorrow.[13]

---

[13] Ibid., p. 64.

ACT 1, SCENE 16 - PILGRIMS VISITING

NARRATORS COME TO SPEAK AT THE SIDE OF STAGE AS ACTION ON STAGE IS THE ARRIVAL OF SPECTATORS FOR THE APPARITION. VILLAGERS SOME IN BETTER CLOTHING – OTHERS JUST SIMPLE PEASANTS WALKING WITHOUT SHOES LOOKING FOR THE CHILDREN. THESE TWO OLDER MEN ARE PRIESTS AND A RELIGIOUS SISTER OR TWO HAVE COME SEARCHING FOR THE SITE OF THE APPARITION. MOST ARE CARRYING A SIMPLE BAG WITH FOOD AND DRINK FOR THE JOURNEY. MOST HAVE A LONG WOODEN WALKING STAFF.

NARRATOR 1:   The story has spread and so there are curious people.

NARRATOR 2:   Some believers too. At least thirty or forty.

NARRATOR 1:   Yes, coming to see if anything out of the ordinary is going to happen at the Cova da Iria.

FATHER JOE: The news spread quickly to the surrounding villages, Sam.

SAM: I think some of these people, these visitors, really believed the children's story.

FATHER JOE: You are right, Sam, I'm sure too. Just remember Sam, we are hearing Our Lady speak as the story goes on. But one hundred years ago only Lucia and Jacinta HEARD Our Lady speaking.

ACT 1, SCENE 17 - COVA DA IRIA

JUNE 13: COVA DA IRIA - EXTRA PEOPLE - NEED NOT BE TOO CROWDED. THE ANGELUS BELL IS HEARD AS THE CURTAIN OPENS AND THE CHILDREN ARE KNEELING PRAYING QUIETLY SAYING THE FINAL PRAYERS. THE SMALL CROWD IS EXCITED AND CHATTING AMONGST THEMSELVES. AS THE BRIGHT LIGHT COMES ACROSS THE VALLEY AND THE SMALL CLOUD SETTLES OVER THE TREE AS OUR LADY APPEARS CROWD IS SILENT AND ATTENTIVE.

LUCIA: Please be quiet. (GESTURES TO CROWD) Please be quiet.

LUCIA: Thank you for coming, dear Lady. Thank you. What do you expect of me, dear Lady?

OUR LADY: I want you to come here on the 13 July and the 13th day of all the months through to October.

LUCIA AND JACINTA: Oh yes, we want to come.

OUR LADY: You should learn to read. And please pray the Rosary every day.

LUCIA: Our friend Mr Sarto has been sick. "Please Lady, will you heal him?"

OUR LADY: Mr Sarto is looking for God; seeking God. If he comes to believe, if he accepts God's message and is received into the church, yes then he will be healed before the end of the year.

LUCIA: Dear Lady, will you please take us three children to heaven?

OUR LADY: Yes. I shall take Jacinta and Francisco soon. But you must stay here for some time.

LUCIA: Oh dear Lady, will I be alone?

OUR LADY: No, no. You will stay here because Jesus wishes you to make me known and loved.

LUCIA: Yes, I will try.

OUR LADY: Jesus wants people to come to know and love Him through the devotion to His Sacred Heart and my Immaculate Heart.[14]

LUCIA: Yes. (NODDING)

OUR LADY: Jesus wishes the devotion to the Immaculate Heart to be established throughout the world. You will come to understand what is to be done. I will help you.

OUR LADY OPENS HER HANDS AND THE LIGHT STREAMS FROM HER PALMS ENGULFING THE CHILDREN WHO ARE ABLE TO SEE THE IMAGE OF THE SACRED HEART AND THE IMMACULATE HEART OF MARY. THE LEAVES ON THE SMALL TREE RUSTLE AS THE BREEZE AND THE VISION MOVES OFF INTO THE SKY. SHE IS GOING.

LUCIA: She is going, she is leaving (POINTING) look … see the clouds are opening and now she is entering heaven. Now the doors are shut.[15]

CROWD ERUPTS WITH EXCITEMENT AND QUESTIONS. LOUDLY AND ALL TOGETHER:

1ST BYSTANDER: What did she say?

2ND BYSTANDER: Is it the Virgin Mary?

3RD BYSTANDER: Is she coming again?

---

[14] Ibid., p. 68.

[15] Ibid., p. 69.

4TH BYSTANDER: I could feel the breeze and hear a buzzing sound. (TAKING LEAVES OFF THE TREES WHERE OUR LADY STOOD.)

BYSTANDERS REPEAT ALL QUESTIONS NOISILY.

CHILDREN GROUP TOGETHER

JACINTA: The Lady told us to say the Rosary every day.

LUCIA: And to pray for peace.

FRANCISCO: She was very beautiful and so sad.

LUCIA: Please do not take all the green leaves from the small tree. This is a special place.

MORE QUESTIONS REPEATED

JACINTA: Nothing else.

FRANCISCO: She is beautiful and so sad. Please, we have to get home. The Lady wants everyone to say the Rosary often.

CROWD DISPERSE. SCENE CHANGES.

ACT 1, SCENE 18 - MARTO'S HOME

MARTO'S HOUSE JACINTA AND FRANCISCO BURST IN EXCITEDLY; OTHER CHILDREN - JOHN AND ANNA CARRYING WHITE BREAD HAVE BEEN TO THE FIESTA AND MUMMA AND POPPA HAVE RETURNED HOME WITH TWO OXEN FOR THEIR HERD.

JACINTA: (RUNNING IN EXCITEDLY) She came…she came - we saw the beautiful lady!

FRANCISCO: Our Lady came to the Cova again. Plenty of other sticky beaks came too.

OLIMPIA: We are not going to go through all this again.

TI: Now Olimpia, let the children tell us their story. It is something very special and they are bubbling with the excitement.

JACINTA: She is so beautiful and Our Lady told us to say the Rosary every day.

FRANCISCO: And we must pray for sinners. And Jacinta and I are going to Heaven soon.

OLIMPIA: What else did the lady say?

JACINTA: Some things are a secret - we must not tell anyone.

FRANCISCO: So many people came, asking too many questions. We need time to pray not to answer silly questions.

OLIMPIA, VERY BUSINESS-LIKE, PROCEEDS TO PREPARE THE EVENING MEAL AS THE SCENE ENDS.

ACT 1, SCENE 19 - DOS SANTOS HOME

DOS SANTOS HOME

MARIA ROSA:　Do you have more stories to tell today, Lucia. You are making us the laughing stock of all the Serra. And so…did anything happen at the Cova today?

LUCIA:　Yes, Mumma – the beautiful little Lady came to see us again. She asked us to continue to pray the Rosary. I do not want to upset you Mumma but it is true. She is so lovely and she said she came from Heaven.

MARIA ROSA:　You are just too much for me, child. I will take you to see Father Ferreira again tomorrow to see if he can get the truth from you.

LUCIA:　The Lady says I should learn to read and write.[16]

MARIA ROSA:　School for you! Indeed. You are ten years old. And who will tend the sheep?

MARIA:　Poor Lucia – she has had visions of her own to try to convince Mumma and Poppa to send her to school.

GLORIA:　Pity she didn't stay at the Fiesta and join in the dancing and singing. It may have brought her out of her dream - brought her to her senses!

SCENE ENDS

CURTAIN

NEXT MORNING MARIA ROSA AND LUCIA ARE OFF TO SEE FATHER FERREIRA.

---

[16] Ibid., p. 72.

ACT 1, SCENE 20 - ST. ANTHONY'S CHURCH

FATHER FERREIRA: Come this way Lucia. Take a seat Mrs Dos Santos.

MARIA ROSA SITS IMPATIENTLY OUTSIDE WHILE THE QUESTIONING IS CARRIED OUT. PAUSE. FATHER FERREIRA AND LUCIA REAPPEAR. LUCIA, VERY DOWN AND LOOKING SAD AND DEPRESSED.

FATHER FERREIRA: It does not seem like a revelation from heaven to me. I think it may be a deception of the devil.[17] We shall see! We shall see! We shall give our opinion later on.

MARIA ROSA: Thank you Father. Good-day Father. On your way. Lucia. (WITH A PUSH)

CURTAIN

---

[17] Ibid., p. 75.

ACT 1, SCENE 21 - FRONT OF CURTAIN

NARRATOR 1:   The children are learning something about suffering.

NARRATOR 2:   They are determined to pray for sinners and offer all their sufferings for sinners.

FATHER JOE AND SAM ENTER.

SAM: They must be sick of people asking them questions!

FATHER JOE: Yes and they try to avoid the visitors who are so curious. Remember Sam – we are all tonight hearing what Our Lady said to the children. Way back in 1917 when it all happened the people could not even see Our Lady. They could follow some of what Lucia said.

SAM: The people knew something very special was happening.

FATHER JOE: Oh yes – they felt the cool breeze – they saw the clouds moving – they saw the leaves on the little tree move. Some saw the reflection of light on the children's faces.

SAM: All the people were very quiet when Our Lady was there. They knew something very special was happening.

AS FATHER JOE AND SAM MOVE TO LEAVE THE STAGE

FATHER JOE: The children tried to avoid meeting with any visiting priests who come to the village of Fatima, because the priests have more questions than others.

SCENE CHANGES

ACT 1, SCENE 22 - OUTSIDE RURAL SCENE

OUTSIDE IN A SHADY AND QUIET AREA – LUCIA, JACINTA AND
FRANCISCO ARE PLAYING SOME SIMPLE GAME.

JACINTA: Poppa is very sensible. He believes we are telling the truth.
             (TURNING TO LUCIA) Lucia, you are not having a nice time at
             home.

LUCIA: No, no one gives me any rest. I try to stay in my room so I can pray.
             I really wonder how I will get the message out to all the world as
             the Lady asked me.

FRANCISCO: You will. Our Lady will help you - she came back in June and she
             will come again on the 13th of every month for the next (COUNT
             ON FINGERS) four months. Maybe then she will take Jacinta and
             I to heaven.

JACINTA: That would be wonderful!

FRANCISCO: Here Lucia, Jacinta. I found this piece of rope the other day and I
             have cut it into three pieces. I think we should wear it next to our
             skin.

LUCIA: It would be very uncomfortable!

FRANCISCO: Yes, it is. I have tried it. It would be a special sacrifice. It is something
             we could offer to Jesus to console Him.

JACINTA: Oh, yes yes. We would be making a sacrifice for sinners to console
             Jesus and Mary.

LUCIA: What a great idea. We will start today. (PAUSE TO TIE ROPE
                 AROUND THE WAIST NEXT TO THE SKIN – ALL THREE
                 CHILDREN SHOW SIGNS OF DISCOMFORT. LUCIA
                 CONTINUES, POINTING): But look - quickly. See in the
                 distance – two priests coming – quickly get behind the bushes.
                 And hush!

PRIESTS WITH FOOD BAGS HATS AND WALKING CANES WALK BY AS
THE CHILDREN HIDE. PRIESTS LEAVE STAGE.

CHILDREN COME FROM BEHIND BUSHES.

LUCIA: The Priests are the ones who ask more questions than all the
                 others. Priests should know we are telling the truth.

THE CHILDREN STROLL ALONG WHEN SUDDENLY THEY ARE
APPROACHED FROM BEHIND BY A GROUP OF VISITORS.

1ST VISITOR: Hello there – if you please could you direct us to the homes of the
                 three children who believe they have seen Our Lady?

FRANCISCO: Continue down this path, at the fork go to the right and you will
                 soon come to the Marto home - it has a white door.

LUCIA: The Dos Santos home will be just another few minutes further on.

2ND VISITOR: Thank you children.

JACINTA: It is not too far away – about ten minutes to go.

VISITORS CONTINUE ON THEIR WAY, THANKING THE CHILDREN AS
THEY GO.

THE 3 CHILDREN SKIP AWAY WITH DELIGHT AND CONTAIN THEIR
JOY UNTIL THE VISITORS ARE OFF STAGE.

FRANCISCO: We could not tell a lie!! (AS THE CHILDREN LAUGH
                        MERRILY.)

CURTAIN / SHORT BREAK. CHILDREN REMAIN IN PLACE.

ACT 1, SCENE 23 - FRONT OF CURTAIN

FATHER JOE: Visitors came to try to speak with the children at any time during the month. They had so many questions – the children became clever at recognising strangers and quickly avoided them when possible.

SAM: Today is the twelfth of July - there will be so many more visitors looking for the children today and tomorrow.

CURTAIN REOPENS

LUCIA: I hate to think about the visit to the Mayor of this Province. He is coming to the Cova this month. He wants to see for himself, just what is going on. He wants to ask us questions too. (VERY WORRIED AND WALKING AWAY FROM THE OTHER TWO CHILDREN.)

JACINTA: We will have to suffer all that for the love of Jesus.

FRANCISCO: And we must pray for peace in the world.

LUCIA: Yes. But Father Ferreira said it might be a trick of the devil.

JACINTA: It's not the devil. The devil is fowl and ugly and he is under the ground in hell. (STAMPING HER FEET LOUDLY). Our Lady is beautiful and kind. We saw her go up to Heaven.

FRANCISCO: Look here! We don't have to be afraid of anything. The Lady is our friend. She will always help us!

LUCIA: No, I have not been able to sleep properly since Father Ferreira said it could be a trick of the devil. I am NOT going tomorrow.[18]

_____

[18]   Ibid., p. 77.

FRANCISCO: How can you think it was the devil? Didn't you see Our Lord and
                Our Lady in the great light?

LUCIA: I'm not going. I'm NOT going.

JACINTA: Well I am going. Nothing can stop me.

FRANCISCO: Me too. I could not let that beautiful little Lady down.

CURTAIN

NEXT DAY MARIA ROSA LOOKING OUT HER FRONT WINDOW AS
PEOPLE TRAVELLING TO THE COVA PASS BY.

ACT 1, SCENE 24 - WINDOW OF DOS SANTOS HOUSE

MARIA ROSA: All these curious people. They *think* they will be in for a surprise today. (SHE IS VERY SATISFIED AS SHE HAS NOT SEEN LUCIA HEADING OFF WITH THE SHEEP TO THE COVA.)

ACT 1, SCENE 25 - FRONT OF CURTAIN

NARRATOR 1:   Lucia's mother is pleased - but where is Lucia.

NARRATOR 2:   She cannot stay at home. She is running off to the Marto home.

NARRATOR 1:   And there she finds Jacinta and Francisco kneeling by the bed praying and weeping.

LUCIA: What are you two doing here? It is getting near the time of the Angelus.

JACINTA: We have been up all night praying for you.

FRANCISCO: We have been praying that you would change your mind. (SPEAKING TOGETHER) We prayed all night.[19]

LUCIA: Well, your prayers are answered. I've decided to go. We must run quickly or we will be late.

ALL EXIT

AS THE CHILDREN RUN OFF, VISITORS FROM ALL PARTS OF PORTUGAL – SOME VERY WELL OFF AND MANY OTHERS WORKERS AND PEASANTS ALL CROSS THE STAGE DURING THE NARRATION.

NARRATOR 1:   As the crowd gathers for the anticipated apparition, we will take a short interval.

NARRATOR 2:   We will return after the visitors and children arrive at the Cova da Iria.

INTERVAL

---

19   Ibid., p. 77.

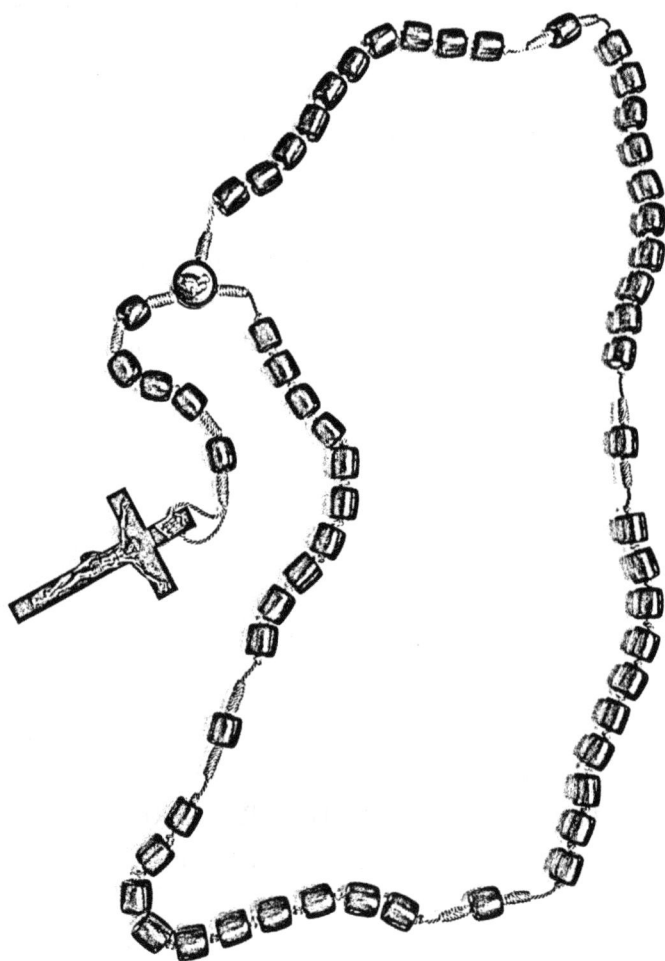

ACT 2, SCENE 1 - FRONT OF CURTAIN

JULY APPARITION

NARRATOR 1:   It is the 13th July, 1917. A crowd of over two thousand people from all walks of life had gathered at the Cova.

NARRATOR 2:   The children had to walk in and out of the visitors on their way to the little oak tree.

NARRATOR 1:   They kneel and hold their rosaries as the Angelus rings out.

FATHER JOE: Look at the crowds. Some of them have been walking for days to get here.

SAM: I think I would believe that something special was really happening. Perhaps some were jealous that they could not see this visitor from outer space?

FATHER JOE: Not a visitor from outer space - those children are talking about a visitor from Heaven. Heaven may seem a long way away but it is not outer space.

SAM: And about the Rosary..those things hanging from your waist – are they Rosary beads?

FATHER JOE: And here is a small set of beads for you – you can say the Rosary too. (FATHER JOE COULD HAND SOME ROSARY BEADS TO CHILDREN IN THE AUDIENCE IF IT IS APPROPRIATE) It is thinking about the life of Jesus on this earth while you say some Our Fathers and Hail Marys. I'll teach you – it's not too difficult.

SAM: These are the counters. (SAM HOLDING UP BEADS AS THEY MOVE TO THE SIDE OF THE STAGE AND SIT)

ACT 2, SCENE 2- COVA DA IRIA

COVA DA IRIA: VERY CROWDED WITH A CROSS-SECTION OF PEOPLE –
PEASANTS, GENTRY, RICHLY DRESSED, CLERGY ETC. MANY WEARING
HATS AND CARRYING FOOD AND CLAY WATER BOTTLES. CHILDREN
WORK THEIR WAY THROUGH THE CROWD TO THE TREE. THEY
KNEEL AND SAY SILENT PRAYERS AS THE ANGELUS BELLS RING.
SOON A FLASH OF LIGHT AND LIGHT BREEZE BLOWS AND THE
WHITE CLOUD APPEARS OVER THE SMALL OAK TREE AS OUR LADY
APPEARS.

LUCIA: Please be quiet - please take off your hats. I see Our Lady already![20]

LUCIA: Lady, oh dear Lady, what do you want of us?

OUR LADY: I want you to come here on the 13th of next month at this time. I
                want you to continue to say the Rosary in honour of Our Lady of
                the Rosary. Pray for peace and the end of the war for she alone will
                be able to help you.

LUCIA: I hope you will tell us, please tell us, who you are and to perform a
                miracle so that everyone will believe that you are from Heaven.

OUR LADY: In October I will tell you who I am and what I wish you to do. And
                I will perform a miracle so that everyone will have to believe.[21]

LUCIA: Many people have asked me to request favours from you. Maria
                Carreira who has been guarding this little shrine and tree – Maria
                has a crippled son?

OUR LADY: I will not cure him, but I will give him a good means to enable him
                to live if he will say his daily Rosary.

---

[20] Ibid., p. 79.

[21] Ibid., p. 80.

LUCIA: And there are many others – the da Gama and Cruz family and Pedro Pena.

OUR LADY: Yes, there are many sick. You must sacrifice yourselves for sinners and say many times: O Jesus, it is for your love and the conversion of sinners. Please pray to make reparation for the sins committed against the Immaculate Heart of Mary.

AS THESE WORDS WERE SPOKEN OUR LADY OPENS HER HANDS AND THE CHILDREN ALL LOOKED DOWN AND SAW THE HORROR OF HELL. THEY ARE VISIBLY SHAKEN AND HOLD THEIR FACES IN THEIR HANDS.

OUR LADY: You see hell where the souls of poor sinners go. To save them, God wishes to establish the devotion to the Immaculate Heart of Mary. If people do what I tell you, many souls will be saved and there will be peace. But if they do not stop offending God there will be another war, a worse war.

APPARITION CONTINUES BEHIND A LIGHT TRANSPARENT CURTAIN AS FATHER JOE AND SAM COME TO THE SIDE OF STAGE.

ACT 2, SCENE 3 - FRONT OF STAGE

FATHER JOE: This was a very long visit from Our Lady. She had very important things to say.

SAM: And is this the time they were told some more things that were to be kept secret?

FATHER JOE: Yes, these three young children were given a vision of hell. So many souls going to hell because they did wicked things during their lives on earth. That was the first secret. The next secret was that there would be another war if people did not repent and say the Rosary. So much trouble would be coming in Russia. Our Lady spoke of Russia spreading her errors through Communism. Little Jacinta had never heard about the big country called Russia. Our Lady also told of terrible danger for a Pope, in the future.

SAM: But these kids were so young… these were sad things Our Lady told them.

FATHER JOE: Yes, but those children were slowly beginning to understand that they were God's messengers and they had to try to spread the messages from Our Lady to all the people.

CURTAIN IS MOVED AND THE APPARITION CONTINUES

ACT 2, SCENE 4 - COVA DA IRIA

OUR LADY: You must not tell anyone at this time about these things, except Francisco. (PAUSE) Here is a little prayer to say after each mystery of the Rosary. "Oh Jesus, forgive us our sins, save us from the fires of hell, lead all souls to Heaven, especially those in need of your mercy."

LUCIA and JACINTA: Oh, Jesus, forgive us our sins, save us from the fires of hell, lead all souls to Heaven, especially those in need of your mercy.[22]

OUR LADY: You can share this prayer with everyone. (OUR LADY BENDS AND SPEAKS SILENTLY TO THE CHILDREN FOR A SHORT TIME BEFORE SHE SMILES AND LEAVES RISING SLOWLY AND DEPARTING TO THE EAST AS USUAL)

LUCIA: See. There she is moving and the clouds are opening. The clouds are opening as the Lady enters Heaven. (STANDS AND POINTS TO THE EAST)

CROWD ERUPTS AND PUSHES IN TOWARDS THE CHILDREN PELTING THEM WITH QUESTIONS. THERE IS MUCH NOISE AND CONFUSION – MOVEMENT AND QUESTIONS. VISITORS ARE TRYING TO GET NEAR THE CHILDREN. CHILDREN SPEAK OVER THE PILGRIMS QUESTIONS

CHILDREN: You must say the Rosary every day. It is a secret. You must confess your sins and pray for forgiveness. There will be a miracle in October. Some people will be cured. Yes the 13th October.

BYSTANDER 1: What did she say?

BYSTANDER 2: When will she come back?

---

[22] Ibid., p. 82.

BYSTANDER 3: Is she going to cure the sick?

BYSTANDER 4: Did she say anything about the end of the war?

BYSTANDER 5: Did you see her? Did you hear anything? Will she cure my son?

THE CROWD MOVES IN TO QUESTION THE CHILDREN NOISILY

CURTAIN CLOSES - ALL IS SILENT

ACT 2, SCENE 5 - FRONT OF CURTAIN

FATHER JOE: Our Lady was with the children a long time. They are exhausted and need to get home quickly.

SAM: Do you think people could feel the presence of someone very special?

FATHER JOE: Oh yes – they could feel the cool breeze and most of them could see the cloud over the small tree. They knew something extraordinary had taken place. They could see some reflection of the light in the children's faces. Oh yes, they knew. (BOTH FATHER JOE AND SAM NOD KNOWINGLY AS THEY LEAVE THE STAGE.)

THIS COULD ALSO BE CHOSEN AS BEING APPROPRIATE FOR INTERVAL.

NARRATOR 1:   By July, the Mayor was fighting mad about the disruption occurring in all the towns and villages near Fatima. By August he was furious. He was part of a government which was against all religions. He wanted to know the secret.

NARRATOR 2:   He was convinced the Catholic Church was plotting with the children against the Government's control. Government officials were shocked by the number of people interested in the Fatima events. Church Officials were also surprised at the attention given to the apparitions.

NARRATOR 1:   The thirteenth of August came and the Mayor took matters into his own hands. Six thousand people had been walking for days to get to Fatima. As the children walked to the Cova, he came along in his car, one of the first cars ever to come to Fatima.

NARRATOR 2:   The Mayor pressured the children to allow him to drive them to the Cova.

NARRATORS 1 & 2: But no - Lucia, Jacinta, and Francisco were taken from Fatima to the Mayor's Office, and then they were put in a common jail with many other prisoners.

MAY INSERT A CAMEO GROUP OF PRISONERS – VERY POOR AND RAGGED - SURROUNDED BY THE THREE CHILDREN. ALL ARE UNITED IN SINGING A SHORT HYMN.

ACT 2, SCENE 6 - MARTO HOME

MARTO HOME. PARENTS GATHER – TI AND OLIMPIA, MARIA ROSA
AND ANTONIO - ALL VERY WORRIED.

OLIMPIA: Our children did not show up near midday at the Cova. Our
                    families are in more trouble with the whole village. They will make
                    fools of us. Everyone is hopping mad at us!

MARIA ROSA: How can we ever show our faces again? Our families were once
                    respected. We will be shamed to death.

TI: We cannot be worrying about ourselves. It's the children we have
                    to be concerned about.

OLIMPIA: John and Anna saw the three of them get into the Mayor's car. The
                    Mayor was looking so kind and helpful but they did not want to go
                    at first.

MARIA ROSA: But they did – and they were taken away. Much to our shame!

ANTONIO: The Mayor would not even speak to me yesterday, when I walked
                    over to try to reason with him. I was not allowed to see my own
                    daughter!

TI: We cannot sit here and do nothing.

MARIA ROSA: It is now over 24 hours since they were taken.

OLIMPIA: There is something Jacinta would say "Pray Mumma - pray for us."

TI: Indeed – but I am going to do more. I will take our donkey and go
                    over to see the Mayor myself.

MARIA ROSA: Antonio has already missed a day's work, and now Ti will not be able to work for the day because he is chasing our troublesome children.

TI: Don't worry about the work Maria Rosa – it's our little ones we have to think about.

CURTAIN

ACT 2, SCENE 7 - MAYORAL OFFICE

MAYOR'S OFFICE: SITTING BEHIND RAISED DESK – CHILDREN HUDDLED TOGETHER STANDING BEFORE HIM.

MAYOR: (YELLING) *You* are causing the trouble – so much trouble and so many disturbances!

LUCIA, JACINTA & FRANCISCO STAND WITH BOWED HEADS, VERY CLOSE TOGETHER.

MAYOR: There is no peace in this whole area for two or three days every month, because of you three! When is it going to cease? (PAUSE - THEN ANSWERING HIMSELF) I know! (BANGING THE DESK) Now – from this day forward! Once you tell me the secret, it will be all over!

LUCIA: No Sir, we will not tell you the secret.

MAYOR: Speak up. Speak up – what are you saying? The village of Fatima is a shambles - the fields are being ruined with people walking all over the crops. There is not enough food and water for the crowds who foolishly keep turning up! How can people be so stupid?

JACINTA: We do not ask them to come.

MAYOR: Be quiet child! Don't speak nonsense! You three are the cause of all the trouble. Telling stories about a beautiful Lady.

FRANCISCO: (VERY BRAVELY AND FIRMLY) It is true Sir – she is a beautiful Lady and she told us she comes from Heaven.

MAYOR: You can go on telling those stories if you wish. Tell stories! All
                I want to know is the secret! Well, what's the great secret? I have
                given you many chances and now I am telling you this - YOU ARE
                NOT LEAVING HERE ALIVE UNLESS YOU TELL ME THE
                SECRET.

CHILDREN TURN THEIR HEADS AND HOLD EACH OTHER.

MAYOR RINGS THE BELL ON HIS DESK IMPATIENTLY. ATTENDANT
ENTERS.

MAYOR: Is the oil good and hot?

ATTENDANT: (VERY LOUDLY) Yes Sir.

MAYOR POINTS TO JACINTA.

MAYOR: Step forward Miss. This is your last chance young lady - tell me the
                secret!

JACINTA: I will not tell. Our Lady asked me not to tell anyone.

MAYOR: Take her away. Throw her in the boiling oil!

ATTENDANT TAKES JACINTA AND SHE IS PULLED TO THE DOOR.

ATTENDANT: Yes Sir.

LUCIA AND FRANCISCO HUDDLE TOGETHER AND GRASP HANDS
TOGETHER IN PRAYER.

MAYOR: Maybe you two will be sensible now. Here boy! Come here! Tell me the secret.

FRANCISCO: I will not. Our Lady has told us not to tell anyone.

MAYOR: I am losing my patience. This is your last chance. Tell me the secret!!

FRANCISCO: I am sorry Sir, I cannot tell you the secret.

MAYOR: (RINGS THE BELL) Here's another foolish child. Throw him into the oil too.

ATTENDANT TAKES FRANCISCO ROUGHLY.

MAYOR: (MORE GENTLY AND IN A PERSUADING MANNER)
                Here Lucia. Now you are a bit older and certainly must have more sense than your cousins. Surely you can tell me, the Mayor, the secret?

LUCIA: I'm sorry Sir, I cannot tell you.[23]

MAYOR: Foolish child. You are throwing your life away like your crazy cousins. (RINGS THE BELL)

ATTENDANT: Yes Sir.

MAYOR: Wait until the oil gets extra hot – this one should have had more sense!

CURTAIN

---

[23] Ibid., p. 113.

ACT 2, SCENE 8 - FRONT OF CURTAIN

FATHER JOE: This was an awful experience for the children.

SAM: Yes, I think I would have told the Mayor the Secret.

FATHER JOE: You are honest Sam. (PATTING SAM ON THE HEAD) These
                children were praying all the time so that they would be strong and
                keep the secret.

SAM: They must have been very scared to be taken away from their
                parents!

FATHER JOE: Yes, they were scared. But their prayers helped them through the
                terrible time.

SAM: Yes. I guess you are right, Father.

NARRATOR 1:   The children were held overnight. The Mayor questioned them
                again the next day.

NARRATOR 1 & 2: They did not break their promise. They did not reveal the secret.

NARRATOR 2:   The Mayor then ordered the clerk to take them back to Fatima.

REUNION WITH PARENTS:
CLERK IS SEEN WITH CHILDREN WHO ARE EXCITED TO SEE THEIR
HOMES AGAIN. PARENTS AND CHILDREN GATHER OUTSIDE THE
CHURCH IN THE SQUARE – FLEXIBLE PLACE FOR UNION.

ACT 2, SCENE 9 - RURAL SETTING

SUNDAY 19 AUGUST, 1917.
APPARITION: SUNDAY AFTER MASS LUCIA MEETS FRANCISCO AND JOHN WALKING OUT TO THE SHEEP. A LOVELY SUNNY MORNING AND AS THEY WALK, LUCIA IS SUDDENLY AWARE THAT THE ATMOSPHERE IS CHANGING.

FRANCISCO: Lucia, come with John and I out to check on the sheep. Jacinta is still at home.

JOHN: Let's get to the shade- it is too hot here in the sun.

LUCIA: (EXCITEDLY) I can feel the atmosphere changing. I think the Lady is going to come. John, please run back for Jacinta.

John: It's too hot. I don't want to go back in this heat.

Lucia: Here is a penny – (PLEADING) please go for Jacinta and tell her to come quickly.

JOHN GOES RELUCTANTLY BUT SOON JACINTA IS ON HER WAY. THE TREES WERE SHIMMERING WITH THE BRIGHT LIGHT AND SOON ON TOP OF A SMALL TREE THE BEAUTIFUL LADY WAS STANDING.

LUCIA: Dear Lady – thank you for coming. I am sorry we could not come on the thirteenth. We really tried.

OUR LADY: I understand.

LUCIA: Please tell me what I am to do for you?

OUR LADY: I want you and your cousins to go to Cova da Iria on the thirteenth day of September and October. Please continue to recite the Rosary every day. In October, I will perform the miracle so that all will believe.

LUCIA: Thank you, dear Lady. (PAUSE) What about the money the people have left at the Cova?

OUR LADY: Make two carriers for the statues. You and Jacinta will carry one with two more girls dressed in white. The other is for Francisco and three other boys to carry. The money will help to build a chapel which they are going to have built.[24]

LUCIA: Dear Lady, I want you to cure some sick people.

OUR LADY: Yes, some I will cure some during the year. Pray, pray a great deal for sinners. Many could go to hell because they have no one to make sacrifices and to pray for them.

OUR LADY, SMILING AND BENDING TO THE CHILDREN. OUR LADY RISES FROM THE TREE AND DEPARTS ACROSS THE SKY. THE CHILDREN RISE SLOWLY AND GO TO THE TREE WHERE THEY CUT OFF SOME BRANCHES TO TAKE HOME WITH THEM.

FRANCISCO: Smell the wonderful scent of Heaven. Our Lady has left us a wonderful gift.

JACINTA: Let's take some branches home. It's like a mini miracle!

LUCIA: Maybe even Mumma will be a little pleased if she smells this.[25]

CHILDREN ALL EXIT IN A CONTEMPLATIVE WAY, NOTICING THE WONDERFUL FRAGRANCE OF THE BRANCHES THEY ARE CARRYING.

MID CURTAIN

---

[24] Ibid., p. 120.

[25] Ibid., p. 121.

ACT 2, SCENE 10 - FRONT OF CURTAIN

FATHER JOE: Our Lady did come in August to console the children who were learning something about suffering. They had an awful time with the Mayor.

SAM: I'm pleased Our Lady came in August. Those kids were so good and strong.

FATHER JOE: They were scared and worried but they prayed – they asked Jesus to help them. They offered their sufferings as a prayer for sinners, and to make reparation to the Sacred Heart of Jesus.
EXIT

NARRATOR 1: Visitors were coming and going to Fatima at any time during the month.

NARRATOR 2: As the 13th of September drew near the prayerful pilgrims and the curious others became greater in number.

ACT 2, SCENE 11 - OUTSIDE MARTO HOME

LUCIA, JACINTA AND FRANCISCO GATHER OUTSIDE MARTO'S HOUSE

JACINTA: Look at the people coming to go to the Cova.

FRANCISCO: They all have so many questions. They want to know the colour of
                 Our Lady's clothes, how she holds her Rosary Beads.

LUCIA: I am shocked when they ask me to tell them the secret. And so
                 many Priests expect me to break my promise to the Lady.

A GROUP OF PILGRIMS APPROACH QUICKLY AND ONE THROWS
HERSELF DOWN AT LUCIA'S FEET. SOON AFTER A SECOND PILGRIM
IS KNELLING AT LUCIA'S FEET.

PILGRIM 1:   Please, please, ask Our Lady to cure my daughter who is blind?

PILGRIM 2:   And will you ask Our Lady to bring my two sons home from the
                 war?

LUCIA: (HELPING BOTH TO THEIR FEET) Yes, yes, but the Lady says
                 you must say the Rosary every day and pray and make sacrifices for
                 poor sinners.

JACINTA: Come Lucia, we have to move along.

FRANCISCO: Do come with us. We are going to the Cova now. We will be caught
                 up with the crowds.

AS THEY MOVE TO EXIT THEY ARE FOLLOWED BY PEOPLE WHO ARE
HEADING TO THE COVA.

ACT 2, SCENE 12 - COVA DA IRIA

SEPTEMBER 13: APPARITION. BIG CROWD SCENE. SUGGEST THIS CROWD IS READY FOR SEPTEMBER AND OCTOBER APPARITION WITHOUT ANY CHANGES. UMBRELLAS AND RAIN COATS FOR OCTOBER HIDDEN DURING THE SEPTEMBER APPARITION.
AT THE COVA DA IRIA: CHILDREN ARE IN POSITION FOR THE APPARITION. THEY KNEEL AND COMMENCE THE ROSARY AND THE CROWD JOINS IN PRAYER.

LUCIA, JACINTA AND FRANCISCO: Hail Mary, full of grace the Lord is with Thee, Blessed art Thou among women and Blessed is the fruit of your womb Jesus.

CROWD: Holy Mary Mother of God Pray for us sinners, now and at the hour of our death. Amen.

LUCIA, JACINTA AND FRANCISCO: Oh my God I believe in you, I adore you, I hope in you and I love you, I ask pardon for those who do not believe, do not adore, do not hope and do not love you.

FLASH OF LIGHTNING AND LIGHT, OUR LADY APPEARS AND MOVES TO TOP OF THE TREE, SMALL CLOUD UNDERNEATH HER FEET, AND ABSOLUTE SILENCE.

LUCIA: Thank you dear Lady. Thank you for coming. My Lady – what do you want of me?

OUR LADY: My children, please continue to say the Rosary to bring about the end of the war. In October, Saint Joseph with the Child Jesus will come to bless the world. You are offering many sacrifices which please God. Do not wear the rope during the night. It is enough to wear it each day.

LUCIA: So many people have begged me to ask you to cure their sick, and
                    some ask to bring their children back to God.

OUR LADY: Some I will cure. In October, I will perform a miracle so that all
                    will believe.[26]

LUCIA: Look she is going. (POINTING TO THE CLOUDS) See the
                    clouds open and she is gone!

NOISE AND CHATTER FROM EVERYWHERE. THE CHILDREN ARE
CLASPED BY THE PILGRIMS AND THE QUESTIONS CONTINUE.

MEMBERS OF THE CROWD ASK: Did you ask about my son at the war?
                    What colour is the Lady's dress? Is she holding anything in her
                    hands? What did she say? Is she coming again? When can we see
                    the miracle?

TI: Come children, come with me. Make way please. The children
                    must get home. Make way please.

---

[26] Ibid., 128.

ACT 2, SCENE 13 - FRONT OF CURTAIN

NARRATOR 1:   After the tumultuous September apparitions, there is no peace for the children or their families. Pilgrims come nearly every day to look for them.

NARRATOR 2:   The children continue with their usual duties, but rise very early to take the sheep to different places where they may be able to get some peace to pray a little.

FATHER JOE: The September visit was wonderful for many people. They have written how they saw the globe of light moving and settling on the little tree.

SAM: Who were these people, Father Joe?

FATHER JOE: Many were locals - some clergy and some not Catholics - they came and many of the holy people who had been coming every month, and they reported what they saw. They really believed the children's story. Many believed that Our Lady had been speaking with the children.

SAM: I hope those believers told the children they had faith in their stories about Our Lady speaking to them.

FATHER JOE: I think they would have Sam.

ACT 2, SCENE 14 - INSIDE DOS SANTOS HOME

DOS SANTOS HOUSE. ANTONIA AND MARIA ROSA ARE JUST FINISHING BREAKFAST.

ANTONIO: I am worried about our crops. Nothing can be planted at the Cova da Iria now that we can expect a crowd there for these so-called apparitions. I will have to rely on Ti Marto to supply our vegetables this year.

GLORIA: We won't even be able to pick wild flowers at the Cova. Everything has been trampled upon. And now it is all mud and slush.

ANTONIO: It is still raining and so muddy everywhere. Yet I have to go to the Cova today to see the destruction of my farm and to see if anything special happens. (EXITS)

MARIA ROSA: Your father is so angry – his potato crop is ruined already. Here we are in October and there is a bigger crowd of people walking to the Cova.

GLORIA: The ground will be worse than useless for any crop. How will we get through winter?

MARIA OF THE ANGELS: Lucia has been so very determined. She has not stopped to think of the problems for our family when there is nothing to sell to the market - nothing to sell and so nothing to bring home to eat. (THROWING HANDS ABOUT)

GLORIA: (POINTING) Look at the number of people arriving already. They have been coming for days.

MARIA ROSA: Nothing will matter much anyway. What if there is no miracle? This crowd is coming for a miracle! No miracle and we will be killed! The three children and any of us who are with them!

LUCIA: (ENTERS) Oh Maria, and Gloria, please wear your white dresses and carry the statue with Jacinta and I today. I would be so sad if you did not come.

MARIA OF THE ANGELS: I will come. But I am not happy about the whole thing. What will become of our family if there is no miracle?

LUCIA: The Lady has promised us a miracle that will make everyone believe. And she will tell us who she is. The Lady will keep her promise. Jacinta and Anna are all dressed in white as well. You will make me so happy if you come.

ACT 2, SCENE 15 - COVA DA IRIA

COVA DA IRIA: IT IS RAINING. ALL UMBRELLAS ARE UP. CROWD IS
BUZZING WITH EXCITEMENT AT THE COVA. THE CROWD COULD BE
SINGING AVE, AVE, AVE MARIA. THE CHILDREN ARRIVE IN THEIR
WHITE DRESSES CARRYING THE STATUE, AND GO TO THEIR USUAL
SPOT NEAR THE TREE. THEY BEND THEIR HEADS TO PRAY. PILGRIMS
SPEAK AND SHOUT OVER EACH OTHER ANXIOUSLY.

LUCIA FRANCISCO AND JACINTA: Hail Mary full of grace, the Lord is
with Thee, Blessed Art Thou among women and blessed is the
fruit of your womb Jesus;

PILGRIMS: Holy Mary, Mother of God, pray for us now, and at the hour of
our death. Amen

PILGRIM: (SHOUTING-INTERUPTING) It is past twelve o'clock!! Where
is the miracle?

FARMER: We must be crazy – here in this hell-hole – covered in mud -
waiting..waiting for what?

PILGRIM: Try to be kind. Just a little longer. Please. Try to be patient!

PILGRIM: The sun is at its peak. When do we see the miracle? We came for
the miracle!

PILGRIM: (LOUDLY) How can you see through the rain and clouds?

PILGRIM: (LOUDLY) Just be patient and say your prayers! Oh ye of little
faith!

LUCIA: (STANDING) Please put down your umbrellas and take off your
hats. Please put down the umbrellas and take off your hats!

THE CROWD SETTLES VERY SLOWLY UNTIL A CRACK OF LIGHTING AND FLASH OF LIGHT WHICH BRINGS SILENCE. THE VIRGIN MARY APPEARS, CLOUD UNDER HER FEET. FLOWERS COVER THE AREA AROUND THE SMALL TREE.

LUCIA: We are so pleased to see you. Thank you for coming. Thank you. Please tell us your name.

OUR LADY: I am the Lady of the Rosary. I want you to continue to pray the Rosary every day.

LUCIA: And all these people are here because they expect a miracle.

OUR LADY: They should try to say the Rosary every day and confess their sins. I will help you spread the message.

LUCIA: Thank you dear Lady. I will do my best.

OUR LADY: And I would like to have a chapel built here in honour of Our Lady of the Rosary.[27]

LUCIA: Yes, I will ask our Parish Priest to tell the Bishop about that.

OUR LADY: The people should be encouraged to have devotion to the Sacred Heart of Jesus and to my Immaculate Heart. Those who embrace these devotions will gain salvation.

LUCIA: Thank you dear Lady. I have many petitions that people have given me – some have asked for cures, others have asked for conversion of sinners.

OUR LADY: Some I will cure, and some not. Our Lord is offended by many sins. People can repent. They can pray for forgiveness of sins. They can see the Priests for confession. They can seek Reconciliation.

---

[27] Ibid., p. 144.

LUCIA: And the war. Please bring peace to the world.

OUR LADY: The war will end soon and the soldiers will return home.

LUCIA: Thank you dear Lady, thank you.

AS OUR LADY OPENS HER HANDS THERE ARE STREAMS OF LIGHT
GOING UP TOWARDS THE SUN. LUCIA STANDS AND POINTS.

LUCIA: Look at the sun! Look up!

THERE IS A SCENE OF THE HOLY FAMILY, MARY IN BLUE AND SAINT
JOSEPH HOLDING THE CHILD JESUS ON HIS ARM.

LUCIA: Saint Joseph is going to bless us! And the Baby Jesus is blessing
                    us![28]

ANOTHER SCENE OF OUR LADY OF SORROWS AND THEN A THIRD
VISION OF OUR LADY OF MT CARMEL WITH JESUS ON HER KNEE.
THESE SCENES PASS FAIRLY QUICKLY AND ATTENTION IS TURNED TO
THE SUN - BRIGHT BUT ABLE TO BE SEEN BY ALL AS IT TURNED IN THE
HEAVENS. THERE ARE STREAMS OF MULTI COLOURED RAYS COMING
FROM THE SKY ACROSS THE CROWDS UNTIL THE SUN PAUSED. THEN
THE SUN APPEARS TO COME AT GREAT SPEED TOWARDS THE EARTH.
EVENTUALLY THE SUN RESUMES ITS PLACE IN THE HEAVENS.

PILGRIMS: SHOUT AND CALL WITH LOUD VOICES CONTINUOUSLY.
                    AS THE SUN APPEARS TO FALL TOWARDS EARTH MANY
                    BECOME FRIGHTENED.

PILGRIM 1:   Miracle, Miracle. Blessed be God.

---

[28] Ibid., p. 145.

PILGRIM 2:   Save us Lord. Save us Jesus.

PILGRIM 3:   Mary, come to save us.

PILGRIM 4:   Blessed be the Virgin Mary!

PILGRIM 5:   O Lord - great is your power!

PILGRIM 6:   Oh my God I am very sorry that I have sinned against you.

PILGRIM 7:   What did you see? I thought it was the end of the world.

PILGRIM 8:   Miracle, Miracle. Jesus help me!

WHEN THE SUN SETTLES, THE CROWD IS SUDDENLY SILENT.
PILGRIMS NOTICE THAT THEIR CLOTHES ARE DRY AND THEY
PROCEED TO MOVE AWAY FROM THE COVA IN AN ORDERLY WAY.

PILGRIMS SPEAKING MORE QUIETLY AS THEY GATHER THEIR
BELONGINGS TO LEAVE.

PILGRIMS 1 & 2:   My clothes are dry – I feel warm and comfortable.

PILGRIMS 3 & 4:   It was a great miracle. It was the Virgin Mary. She came from
                     heaven.

PILGRIMS 5 & 6:   It was Our Lady. We had a visit of the Virgin Mary. She came
                     to Fatima.

PILGRIMS 7 & 8:   The children were telling the truth. The children were telling
                     the truth!

THE MARTO AND DOS SANTOS FAMILIES WITH THEIR CHILDREN
REMAIN ON STAGE AND ALL KNEEL TO FACE THE PLACE OF THE
APPARITION. FATHER JOE, SAM AND THE NARRATORS JOIN THEM.

TI: We must thank God for His goodness. Let us all pray the Angel of Portugal's Prayer - (BOWING LOW) My God I believe, I adore, I hope and I love you; I ask pardon for those who do not believe, do not adore, do not hope and do not love you. (NARRATORS COME FORWARD)

NARRATOR 1:   The miracle on 13th October, 1917 is a miracle that was predicted months in advance. The sun dancing in the heavens was seen up to 40 kilometres away. The miracle of the sun was reported in the press of Portugal and other European cities, and the New York Times.

NARRATOR 2:   The war did end soon and the troops returned home. Pilgrims continued to come to Fatima especially on the 13th of each month.

NARRATOR 1:   All three children were questioned separately by many church officials. The Catholic Church officially approved the Fatima apparitions in 1930.

NARRATOR 1:   Francisco and Jacinta did go to heaven soon – Francisco died in 1919 and Jacinta in early 1920. Both were victims of the worldwide influenza epidemic which followed the War.

NARRATOR 2:   Lucia became a Religious Sister – she wrote and retold the Fatima story. Lucia returned to Fatima to accompany the three Popes who visited there. She lived to help make the message of Fatima widely known. Lucia died in February 2005, aged 97 years.

NARRATOR 1:   On 13 May, 2017 in Portugal, Pope Francis raised Jacinta and Francisco to the honour of sainthood. St.Jacinta, pray for us. St Francisco, pray for us. Blessed Lucia is on the way to becoming a saint.

NARRATORS 1 & 2: The message is the same today as it was 100 years ago. Please pray the Rosary and remember we are all pilgrims on the road to heaven.

CURTAIN

END OF PLAY

133 IMMACULATE MARY

LOURDES 65.65 and refrain

Pyrenean traditional melody

Refrain

A - ve, a - ve, a -
- ve Ma - ri - a; a - ve, a - ve, a - ve Ma - ri - a!

Hail Mary

Anon. from the Herberton Hills.

Hail Ma-ry full of grace. The Lord is with Thee.

Bless-ed art Thou a-mong wo men and bless-ed is the fruit of Thy womb

Jes - us Ho - ly Ma - ry Mo - ther of God Pray for us sin - ners

now and at the hour of our death. Ho - ly Ma - ry Mo - ther of God.

Pray for us sin - ners now and at the hour of our death A - men.

www.ingramcontent.com/pod-product-compliance
Lightning Source LLC
Chambersburg PA
CBHW050640150426
42813CB00054B/1136